Crescendo Publishing Presents

Instant Insights on...

BUSINESS

Branding and Website Essentials *for* Entrepreneurs

Melody Hunter

small guides. BIG IMPACT.

Instant Insights On...

Branding and Website Essentials for Entrepreneurs
By Melody Hunter

ISBN: 978-1-944177-45-4 (p)
ISBN: 978-1-944177-46-1 (e)

Crescendo Publishing, LLC
300 Carlsbad Village Drive
Ste. 108A, #443
Carlsbad, California 92008-2999

www.CrescendoPublishing.com
GetPublished@CrescendoPublishing.com

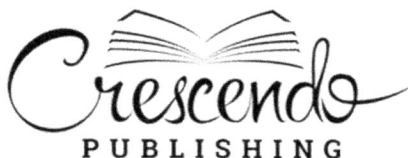

Crescendo
PUBLISHING

What You'll Learn in this Book

In *Branding and Website Essentials for Entrepreneurs* you'll learn how to create a website strategy that sells your services, positions you as an expert, and ultimately grows your business.

When creating your first website, it's easy to let your emotions, your favorite colors, and your personal preferences guide your decisions. However, focusing on your personal preferences leads to confusion and second-guessing.

In *Branding and Website Essentials for Entrepreneurs* I'll teach you what elements really matter and how to make the shift to looking at your website through your visitors' eyes. Trust me—this will not only reduce your stress but make your website much more effective.

You'll get **Instant Insights** on ...

- How to leverage your website to build credibility and authority
- Three keys to increase your online success and achieve your website goals
- A simple exercise to finally understand exactly what pages to include on your website

- How to create your own unique strategy so you obtain leads from your website
- Tips for branding, e-mail marketing, and search engine optimization

A Gift from the Author

To help you implement the strategies mentioned in this *Instant Insights™* book and get the most value from the content, the author has prepared the following bonus gifts we know you will love:

Website XO A Strategic Website Planner:
A fun workbook to play with the ideas and exercises in *Branding and Website Essentials for Entrepreneurs.*

You can get instant access to these complimentary materials here:
http://www.melodyehunter.com/websitexo

Table of Contents

Dedication

For Sierra ♥

What a Website Can Do for Your Small Business

An intentionally designed website can spark a new confidence in your business. Just the act of planning your site will help you to see your business in a new light. Even if your business is just you right now don't make the mistake of thinking you don't need a website.

Can you make money in your business without one? Absolutely! But having a stylish and strategic website makes running your business easier and prettier (that's important).

Are you ready to do business with the world?

Whether you're a copywriter in Dallas, a model in Miami or a social media manager in LA having a website is essential for small business owners and entrepreneurs. If for no other reason than having a website allows you to present your services to the world, you should start creating your site now.

Think about this. You can share your music at the local club or you can upload it to the internet where it can be heard by millions. You can share your makeup tips with your clients in your salon or you can tell the world via your own web presence. Got a great sense of style? Show off your flair for dressing at the mall or blog about your finds to girls all over the globe. Having a website gives your business the ability to do business on a global scale. You can now showcase your products and services to anybody in the world. There are people scattered across the globe who need your help. Make it easy for them to find you.

Do you want to make an impact and have influence?

In addition to opening your business up to the world, having an intentionally created website also positions you as an expert.

Imagine walking into a room and people know who you are before you introduce yourself. A lady walks over to you and shyly says, "I love you. Would you mind taking a picture with me?"

You smile politely and pose for the picture. All the while, you're thinking to yourself, "Holy shift, Me?" A small crowd gathers around you, and people are asking you questions, more people want to take pictures with you. Moments like this are quite possible when you've done the work to create a compelling website.

Your website and blog are the vehicles you use to share your knowledge and expertise with people. When you do that, you create community and a following. Are there things in your industry you wish were different? State that proudly on your website, break the internet, and write a blog post about it.

Sharing your knowledge is helpful in many ways, two of which are:

1. People do repeat business with people, they know, like and trust. The more you share, the more people will get to know you, trust you and want to work with you.

2. Not everyone will be able to hire you, so sharing means caring so sharing your knowledge helps those who are struggling to move forward.

Which brings us to our next point of a having website—creating credibility for your business.

Having a website will give your business credibility, especially if it's very polished and professional and has the correct information on it. A compelling website can make a small Mom and Pop shop look like Nordstrom's, but you've got to have the chops. So be sure to carry the experience over into your work with clients.

Just like a compelling website can do wonders for your credibility, a poorly thought out website can also kill your credibility. Let's be honest. If your site looks cheap, people expect cheap. If your site looks like a knock-off of someone else's people will assume your offers are knock offs too and, of course expect a discount.

Potential clients are going to Google you. Whether someone has just met you at an event or heard about you from a friend if they're thinking about hiring you, they are going to Google you.

Your website should be the first thing people see about your company online. You want to share who you are and what's going on with your business. If you have a stunning website that positions you as an expert, a blog where you share your expertise and showcase and highlight your products and/ or services in a polished, professional way, you boost your credibility. Which is good for business.

I wrote this book to help you plan, write and create a compelling website that builds your brand and helps you make your mark on the world. This book is designed to help you build that credibility and share your expertise on your website. I am going to teach you the essential things that you need as an entrepreneur to put on your website to make sure that your website works as hard as you do.

We will go over several keys to a successful website, including...

- Website terminology so you can talk the talk with designers and programmers.

- Domain and hosting accounts and why this is one of the most important decisions you'll make for your website.

- Web copy, a marketing term for the written word—and they're not just any words. Copy is an art, so we will discuss copy and creating content for your website.

- Branding, which I will simplify it for you, finally.

- We'll deep dive into using a free gift as a lead generation tool.

- I'll walk you through creating your list building sequences. Don't know what this means, keep reading, you will.

- A super-simple SEO plan to optimize your website.

- Finally, we will wrap up by creating your website plan. This is a document and a checklist you will be able to use yourself to begin to create your own website or to pass along to a designer to help you create your website.

Without further ado, let's get started.

Your Instant Insights...

- Having a website is essential for small business owners and entrepreneurs because it gives your business the ability to do business on a global scale.
- A polished, professional website gives your business credibility.
- Share your knowledge and expertise with people. When you do that, you create dedicated and engaged community and a solid following.

Three Keys to a Successful Website

As entrepreneurs providing services there are a few basic essentials that need to be included on your website. Here are three keys that I've found to be essential techniques for having a website that works as hard as you do.

Let's discuss the goals of a successful site. By a "successful site," I mean:

- A website that sells for you
- A website that helps to build your subscriber list
- A website that educates your audience

Imagine that you are at your desk, diligently working on your latest client's project, when your business line rings.

You pick up and on the other line is a friendly voice who nervously asks for you. She has just visited your website and is very interested in working with you.

Yes! It really can be that simple. When you have a website that works, you will get requests to work with you from seemingly out of thin air.

I'm going to walk you through three simple strategies you can use to enhance your website that are key to engaging visitors.

Key #1 – Provide useful, valuable information to visitors.

People online are searching for useful information from experts. Most people who visit your site are not going to buy from you right away, so use your website to share your knowledge and let them know you can help them.

When potential clients land on your site, they are looking for information about you and your services. They want to know more about what you're offering. You can provide this information in the form of articles, a blog, a video, or any form you're comfortable with.

When you're choosing the format for your information, just play to your strengths. If you're not a great writer, use video. If you're not quite ready to step in front of the camera, use audio. The medium is not as important as the message. The main objective here is to share information that visitors are looking for.

This benefits you in two ways: it gives people a reason to visit your site again, and it positions you as an expert.

What is valuable content? Many people get stuck here because they don't want to give away the farm, which you do not have to do. There are many ways to give your visitors valuable content.

You can ...

- Answer common questions
- Explain a complex concept in a way that's easy to understand
- Share information that will help visitors consume your service or product

For example, if your topic is complex, share a tutorial that walks people through the process or include a FAQ section that answers some of your most frequently asked questions. "Value" just means "worth," so when you're developing your valuable content, ask yourself these three questions:

1. Is this worth a visitor's time to read/watch/listen to?
2. Does it address the needs or problems of my target audience?
3. Is it more educational than self-promotional?

When you're using valuable content to promote yourself, just let the information you provide prove it. Inspire people. Motivate and encourage them to take the next step with you.

In order to provide valuable content, you need to know who your audience is, so take the time to clearly define your target audience. Who are you trying to reach? What information are they looking for? And what do you want them to do with this new information you shared?

Key #2 – Invite visitors to keep in touch.

Ask for visitors' contact information so that you can follow up. Building a list of people who are interested in your services is THE best way to jump off the client roller coaster. I'm going to teach you how to implement a lead-generation strategy so that you can start getting leads directly from your website.

Create a Lead Magnet

Unfortunately, most people who visit your site will never visit again. That's why it's important that you invite visitors to stay in touch with you. You want to get their email address so you can follow up with them. The best way to do this is to offer a free gift to visitors. Most people are on your site looking for information, so sharing some of your information to help move you potential client forward is the best thing to offer for free. I like to call this a "freemium" offer or a lead magnet.

Your free offer should meet three criteria:

1. It needs to be valuable and irresistible to your ideal client.
2. It needs to be free (or a very low cost) for you to deliver, and it needs to be able to be delivered immediately to visitors.
3. It needs to position your services as the natural next step for them.

A good example is an audio class, special report, white paper, or video. The medium is not as important as the information.

You'll collect e-mail addresses of your visitors to build a list of people who are interested in working with you. Getting them on the list, however, does not mean they will become clients. It only means they have given you permission to tell them more about your services and what it's like to work with you. Your job is to share and shine. Those who are meant to work with you will, and the others will follow you and learn.

Key #3 – Proudly sell your products and services.

No matter if you offer eyelash extensions or energy healing you'll need to sell your services in order for people to buy them. "Sell" is not a bad thing, it can be done with elegance and authenticity, and—better than that—it can be done without you really "doing" it at all. There are elements you can include on your site to help you effortlessly sell your services with class.

Now when I say 'make you site sell', I mean present your services in a way that creates desire, gives buyers confidence and makes you moo-la.

In order for your site to sell, you need to present your products and services in a compelling way so that buyers want them. Here are the elements you'll need:

- **_Professional Photography_** – A photo is worth a thousand words. It's worth it to invest in professional photography or graphics. The kinds of photos you'll need will vary, but if you're providing professional services a high quality headshot will serve you well. Also don't forget about the power of a great before and after photos.

- ***FAQ*** - Think through questions a potential buyer may have and answer them on your website, be sure to address any additional concerns or objectives.

- ***Testimonials*** - Use testimonials to share results others have had from working with you. There's nothing better then social proof. The more official or realistic your testimonials are, the better. If you can use a picture, full name and a link to a website or Facebook page do it. If you have a sensitive topic like bankruptcy, perhaps initials are expectable.

- ***Payment Processing*** – You'll also need a way to accept payments. There are many services that allow you to put a button on your website or send an invoice via email that will allow your client to pay via credit card. Payment processors like, Square, PayPal, Wave App, Stripe and Freshbooks make it super easy for the little guys to look like the big guys. With clean professional emails.

Your Instant Insights...

- Proudly sell your products and services.
- Invite visitors to keep in touch.
- Provide valuable, relevant information to visitors.

Different Kinds of Websites and When to Use Each

For an entrepreneur who provides professional services there is a general flow and elements visitors will expect to see on your website.

According to Google, a website is "a location connected to the Internet that maintains one or more pages on the World Wide Web."

Your website is a collection of codes that tell your computer how to show things. It is essentially a written file that lists where images should be placed, how elements should be presented, and what functions need to happen.

Each page of your website is connected through your domain name. As an example, your homepage for your site is www.yourwebsite.com.

And each additional page on a website simply adds a backslash and the name of the new page.

Example: www.yourwebsite.com/media

Or www.yourwebsite.com/services

Or www.yourwebsite/contact

You can actually choose those titles for each of the pages as well. When you look at a domain name and it's not a forward slash and a different page at the end, then you are on a new site.

Let's start with the general structure of a website. You can have a strong site with a few simple pages.

Essential Webpages for Your Site

As a service provider you should have the following essential webpages on your site:

- A "Home" or "Welcome!" page explaining who you help and how you help them
- An "About" or "Who We Are" page
- A "Hiring", "Work with Me", or "What We Do" page

INSTANT INSIGHTS ON...BRANDING AND WEBSITE ESSENTIALS FOR ENTREPRENEURS

- A "Contact" or "Interested in Working With Us" page
- A landing page/opt-in page for your free gift. Example: "We're Really Great at What We Do. Here's a FREE sample".

Home Page

Your home page should (1) introduce who you are, (2) clearly explain what you do, and (3) who specifically it is you help. Remember your website is about your potential client, your target audience—to/for whom you provide services. Because your home page is the introduction to your website, you want people to know, as soon as they get there, who you are, what you do, and whether or not you can help them.

Use your home page to present the most important things happening in your business. Special promotions, your lead magnet and glowing testimonials are staples for your home page, but be creative and share something that helps you stand out, perhaps a manifesto.

"About" Page

Your about page is about you, but only as it relates to your reader or ideal client. You want to share with people who you are but not bore them with too much about your dogs and your garden. You want to tell people who you are as it relates to how you can help them. This is also a great place to share things about your journey that have helped you to become someone who can better serve them or who can best help them.

Of course you want to include personal things, but sprinkle them in. Edit with your reader in mind. Be honest with yourself and cut out the boring parts. Your "About" page should focus on your ideal client and your journey as it relates to them.

An "About" page is another great place to include your contact form. I have noticed a trend of including the "About" page and the "Contact" page together, which I think is a really good idea because sometimes the "Contact" page is overlooked. Be sure to include your contact info and at least ways people can contact you.

A phone number is a great idea - You can get a free number or a very inexpensive number that forwards to your phone so that you don't have to share your personal phone number. You can also send those calls to an answering service or to a voicemail, but it's a good idea to have a phone number. Some people will want to call and leave a voice message, or they just want to know they can call and get in touch with someone. Giving them the ability to call and get in touch with you will go a long way.

In addition to a phone number, an address is good too. If you have a physical location, you want to keep your address front and center so that people know exactly where they can find you. There are really cool ways for you to integrate maps or directions through Google onto your website, which also helps with search engines. That's a good option to explore.

So you want to include your phone number, your address, and your contact form so that people can reach out to you. Also include e-mail addresses of any pertinent staff members, assistants, publicists, managers, or whoever handles your speaking engagements.

"Work With Me" Page

Your Work With Me Page is your chance to invite potential clients to take the next step with you. If you offer more than one service, it's a good idea to list all of your services on one page with short descriptions and a button to visit another page on your site that's all about that one service. For example, an author with 3 books may have one book page that lists all 3 books with a short description of each and a button. When a visitor clicks the button they are taken to another page that gives more details about the book.

Here's a nice structure for explaining your offers:

1. Name your offer even if it's a service. Cute names are nice, great names include the

promise of the result. If you go cute use a results based tagline.

2. Tell them exactly what your offer is as simply as possible.

3. Let you readers know you created this for them. Ask questions in your wording that show you understand what problems your ideal clients are having.

4. Share your vision for what's possible for them after working with you.

5. Be specific and share tangible here's what you will get, learn or have after working with you.

6. Walk people through exactly how your offering works and what will happen after they purchase.

7. Share the investment details. How much is your service?

Give people a reason to buy now and call 'em to action. Invite people to take the next step with you. Popular calls to action are: Buy Now, Schedule a Consult, Enroll or Request a Quote.

Don't underestimate the power of a good call to action. If your visitor is interested in working with you, what is that next step you want them to take?

Do you want them to pay for a session right now?

Do you have a price, and can they click a button to pay now?

Do you want them to fill out an application and apply to work with you?

Thinking through your calls to action will help you determine additional needs you may have. For example, you may need to create an application or additional payment buttons. Don't skip this step, slow down and think through your calls to action for your "Work with Me" page.

"Contact" Page

Your "Contact" page is the page on your site that contains all the details of how people can reach you. Typically, an online form is used that visitors can enter their name, email, phone number and a short message into the form. The message is then sent to the website owner via the magic of technology.

Free Gift Landing Page

A landing page that asks for an e-mail address and a name in exchange for your free gift is another important element for entrepreneurs to have on their websites. This is important because most people who stumble across your site will never come back to your site. It's not their responsibility to remember that you're there and they can hire you. It's your job as the entrepreneur to keep yourself on top of their minds. You do that by asking for their information so that you can keep in touch with them.

When you're starting out and want to present your self as polished and professional online, these page will serve you well as you grow your business. So that's it for our general website structure.

Additional Webpages to Add Value

Gallery or Showcase Page

It's important to have a page on your website that displays your work. If you have before-and-after photos, a gallery, or testimonials from clients that can prove or showcase that you can actually do the work, that's an essential page to have.

Speaking or Media Page

Entrepreneurs should also have a "Media" or a "Speaking" page. If you are open to doing some speaking and sharing your knowledge and expertise in front of other people, it goes a long way toward getting clients. Putting together a speaker sheet is great. You can start with one talk or three topics you'd like to speak on. It's also good to have a bio and some information about the audiences that you'd like to reach. Put together a one-sheet and then put it up on the "Media" page. Start to promote yourself as a speaker. As you're promoting yourself, other people will see that, and they will know you're open to speaking. So that's a good page to include.

Frequently Asked Questions (FAQ) Page

An FAQ section is also a good idea. People will always have questions. If you want to limit the number of questions, an FAQ section is an amazing idea. To get started with an FAQ section, when people e-mail you questions, keep them all together in a Google doc or a Word doc and add them to your website as you go. As you answer them, store the answer and the question. Polish them up and start to add them to your website. If other people ask those same questions, you can start to set up a response that sends people directly to your FAQ section.

Let's Talk Blogs.

A blog, which is different from your general website for a few reasons. Where A blog is updated regularly, your general website will typically be updated every six months or once a year.

In contrast, some blogs are updated daily, weekly, or biweekly. A blog can be updated as often as you'd like. Which is one reason search engines love them. Where your general website is more like a book, a blog is more like a magazine. It's short articles that change often, and you can categorize them into sections. Your blog is comprised of many articles, usually 500 – 750 words each. A blog can be a standalone site, or it can be a part of your general website.

One benefit to having a blog is the search engine credibility that you get from it. If you really want to show up on Google for people who are searching for your services or your expertise, blogging is an exceptional way to do that.

You can write articles specifically answering questions that your audience has. When people go to Google, that's how they search—in questions. If you answer questions on your blog, then chances are high that someone will Google one of those questions.

Praise or Testimonials - These should be sprinkled throughout your site, if you have a ton, go ahead and strut your stuff, include a page full of glowing testimonials where people are sharing what they loved about working you.

Other Webpages that Can Stand Alone

In some cases, you may have a requirement for a one-time, stand-alone webpage to support a specific product, service, or event. To accommodate these needs, a single webpage can be a very effective alternative and a lot less work. Here are a few examples:

A product or service sales page is designed exclusively to sell. It's formatting is very structured. There are people who make thousands and thousands of dollars writing one sales letter because it really is that important. Your sales page should be beautiful and functional and sell your services. Investing in good copy for a sales page really is worth it.

A sales page is the page you send visitors to when it's time to purchase. The only purpose of this page is to get visitors to the buy button. There is a real art to the sales page. The copy, or words on the page, and all of the graphic elements are designed and placed strategically to move visitors to your call to action.

An opt-in page is a web page designed to invite visitors to leave their name and email address, often in exchange for a free gift. Typically, this strategy is used to generate leads and as part of a larger email marketing strategy.

A password-protected, private page is a secure webpage that allows access to private content only after payment has been made. Where your general website is open to the public and anyone who types in your domain name (web address) can view it. When you have a membership site, only the people you allow into that site—either by giving them a password or allowing them access after they have paid—can see that content. It's private, protected, members-only content.

Your Instant Insights...

- There are many different kinds of web pages, and there are different reasons for using each kind, so be strategic.
- Search engine credibility is a benefit of a blog.
- It's not your visitors' responsibility to remember your website. It's your job as the entrepreneur to keep yourself top of their minds using an e-mail strategy.

Getting Online: Your Domain Name and Hosting Account

Before you can make your website live on the internet you'll need a hosting account and domain name. Your web host makes it possible for your site to be published on the web. Hosting services work by storing all the files that make up your website on high powered computers connected to lightning fast networks. When a visitor types your website address those computers.

A domain name is essentially your online address. Its what people type in to find your site. My domain name is MelodyHunter.com. Computers actually use a numerical system like 123.456.789, however long strings of numbers are challenging to remember so the use of words as domain name system was created.

You can purchase a domain name through a domain seller like NameCheap or get one through your hosting account provider. Many hosts will provide a free domain name with the purchase of hosting. Hosting is generally purchased annually. Costs for hosting range between about $60 a year to $150 a month depending on the level of service and security your host provides.

It is important to always purchase your own domain name and hosting account and then share that information with your web developer.

Types of Hosting

Shared Hosting: Easy to get started with and fairly inexpensive. With a shared plan your site is stored on a server with many other customer's websites. Think of shared hosting like living in an apartment.

Cloud Hosting: Provides the most flexibility and Cloud hosting is a step up from shared hosting because it allows more security for your website files. With cloud hosting your website files will share the physical servers, however virtual parameters are put in place to protect your site from damaged files and malware that may affect other sites on your server.

Dedicated Hosting: The crème de la crème of hosting, with a dedicated hosting account your site file doesn't share a physical server or resources with any other website you have full control of your server and have the ability to configure it any way you'd like.

Website Builders: Least expensive and least control over, however usually the easiest way to build a website yourself. Typically, a site builder will provide a free domain name that includes the name of their service along with yours.

For example: www.yourwebsite.thirdpartcompany.com instead of www.yourwebsite.com

Your Instant Insights...

- Always own your own domain name.
- Choose a hosting company with world-class security and great customer service.
- Your hosting and your domain name make it possible for your website to be live online.

Creating Content for Your Website

Creating your website will happen in 3 stages.

1. Planning
2. Design
3. Program

Planning Your Website

It's easy to get ahead of yourself and try to jump straight to the design aspects of your website without giving much thought to what words and content will actually need to be included. This oversight can cause major delays with the completion of your website. It's also a huge mistake to ignore this crucial step. **Your content is key to a successful site.**

In marketing terms, we refer to the words you use on your site as "copy," and they are not just any old words. They are marketing words used to create desire for your offer, and answer all questions a potential buyer may have in a compelling way that demonstrates you understand your audience and have created a suitable solution to their problem. Simply put they are words used to sell.

When planning your website, you need to figure out which pages you'll need and what to include on each page.

In this exercise I'm going to show you how to create a site map. A site map is your guide to what pages your site will include and how those pages will link together.

I've created a workbook called Website XO that takes you through an exercise to help you plan your website. Visit MelodyHunter.com/ WebsiteXO to grab your free copy.

The first thing that you want to do when you get ready to build your website is to think through what your goals are.

You'll need to know these three things:

1. You need to be really clear on what it is that you do,

2. You need to be extremely clear on who it is that you serve or who your ideal customer or client is, and

3. You need to know what you want those people to do on your site.

To figure out what pages you'll need on your site think about all the different groups of people who will be visiting your site.

A few examples include: new clients, potential clients, past clients, colleagues, competitors, media. Think through this and list every person who may come to your site.

Once you have a list of all the groups of people who will visit your site, you have to ask yourself, what is the success point for this person who is visiting my site? Where is the point that they have accomplished your goal or their goal, when they have reached that action you want them to take?

For example, a money coach who wants to book more speaking engagements can set a goal for downloads of her media kit. When media planners come to her site, she wants them to download her speaker package and fill out a form to request more information about her speaking.

To achieve this, she will need a:

1. A web page with compelling copy on her site inviting media people to download the speakers kit

2. A speakers one sheet or media kit (these are outside the scope of this book, but a quick Google search will get you going in the right direction.)

3. A web form that emails these requests to her

When you begin to plan your site, it may seem overwhelming, don't let that get you down. A great web designer can make all of those steps super simple. In fact, if this were my client, all she'd have to do is provide the content for the page and the photo and the words for the speaker sheet.

Now that you've thought through these things, you know that you are going to need at least one extra form for speaking engagements only; you will need a speaker's one-sheet plus, you will need the words that go on that speaking page.

Go through these steps for every potential; visitor on your site. Once you know who you are talking to and what the point of that page is creating your copy becomes a lot easier.

Once you have gone through this exercise, you will have an entire list of all the pages you will need on your site and a much better idea of what content you'll need to create or have created for you. Many of the pages on your site will overlap, for example nearly all your visitors will visit your about page and your contact page may be the success point for peers as well as potential clients.

Designing Your Website

Your design is the way the site looks. What fonts, colors and images are used to evoke emotion and make a connection to your audience.

I suggest hiring a web designer, and not because I'm a web designer. Because web design is truly an art form, there are certain colors, fonts and a way to place images and text together that will increase your results. Designers study this. It's like when you wash your hair at home and it looks alright, but then you go to the salon and you walk out hair blowing in the wind and feeling like Selena Gomez in the Pantene commercial. That's the effect good design creates. Also a note about "good design." Good design is subjective, some people love the simplicity of a minimalistic design while other love the chaos of blended colors and wild patterns. When you see good design you know it, it just has a certain polish and remember it's a website, but it's still art. It should make you feel something when you look at it.

Programming Your Website

Yes, programming and design are separate phases of web design. In many cases web designers will only actually design the site for you, not make it work. Programmers are the tech wizzes who come in and actually write the code that makes your buttons click and your sliders slide and your forms submit.

When hiring a web professional, be sure to ask if they will design and build the site or only provide either design or programming.

Your Instant Insights...

- Plan out every page that you need on your site.
- "Copy" refers to words that are created to sell; they are not just any old words.
- Use calls-to-action.

Branding

"Branding" is a trendy word, but it's not really as complex as many people make it out to be. To me, branding has always meant the personification of your business. It's essentially giving your business a personality of its own or infusing your personality into your business. Because it's the personality of your business, it affects so many different aspects, which can make branding confusing. It affects the look and feel of your site: the fonts, the colors, the images, and the messaging. Everything that you say about your business or what you show about your business is a reflection of your brand.

Your brand really is the soul of your business. It's uncovering and unapologetically showcasing your business. You do that by first defining your brand for yourself. If you're creating a personal brand

and you know deeply and truly who you are, it's a lot easier. You can use your own personal traits. You can also use traits of businesses that you love and respect.

For example, I love Google, and Google puts out tons of free, very useful apps like Gmail, Drive and Hangout. All of these things make it really easy for people to connect with technology. I love that. In my brand, if I were to model Google for my brand, I could take some of those traits and create free things that delight and are very useful to my audience.

You can use your own personality and the personalities of other brands, or you can mix and match brands and choose pieces that you like. Say you're like me and you love Taylor Swift. I love Taylor Swift's unapologetically good girl image. She bakes, she loves love and whether she sings it with a country twang or over a glitzy pop track you know it will have beautiful lyrics, a catchy melody and passion. That's branding.

When she releases something, it's going to be good, and it's going to be her style, her flavor. Think about what traits you'd like your brand to exude.

One of the main elements of your brand is a logo. A logo can be really underwhelming for an entrepreneur to see for the first time because some of the best logos are really just a very simple, clean font. It's nothing insane. Think of Nike. Yes, there is a swoosh, but the word "Nike" written out is nothing fancy.

The personality behind the business is what gives meaning to the logo. When you see logos for a movie like *Twilight* or *Harry Potter*, they mean something, and they seem so important and deep because they have an emotional meaning behind them. It's not necessarily the font or the color, even though those things were created with the brand personality in mind and as a reflection of that, which is why it's all so successful.

But their success is not just because of that specific font that they used. I get a lot of entrepreneurs who want to copy. "Just make mine look like so-and-so's," or "I like this one, so can we just use it?" That says a lot about your brand, but it points out to other people that you are not unique. It shows that you are not one of a kind. It shows you are a copycat.

That's not to say that using classic fonts is copying. There is a difference between modeling and copying. To model something is very respected, but to copy it is stealing.

Branding your business is more than consistently using the same fonts and colors, however your visual brand is a reflection of your personality, think about it as your businesses wardrobe.

How do you create a visual brand for your business?

Start with a logo or simple name mark of your company name. Again, your logo does not need to be eccentric. I would suggest using no more than two fonts and no more than two colors, and stay consistent with that. Branding is about being consistent, so that people recognize you and get used to your quality of work.

Don't keep switching: "This week, I like this, and that week, I like that." There will be an evolution as you grow into your business. There will be some changes, but it shouldn't be so drastic that this week it's this font and next week it's something else. You want to get to a point where eventually all your materials are branded and look the same with the same fonts, the same colors, and the same placement of things. People will start to recognize your work from other people. That is what a brand is.

A brand helps to differentiate you from everyone else. When someone sees your work, they know what result they can expect. It's an expected promise.

Your Instant Insights...

- Branding is essentially giving personality to your business.
- Use brand models to help create your own unique mix.
- To model something is very respected, but to copy it is stealing.

Eye-Catching Photos & Illustrations Are Essential

You can have a very beautiful website with only typography design with absolutely no images, using just words, but if you really want to make an emotional connection with someone, the old saying is true, "A picture [or photo or illustration] is worth a thousand words."

One photo can tell someone exactly what you do even if they don't read any words on the site. I see people making a huge mistake by using any image and not thinking about the image that they chose. They need to choose images that go with the wording and the feel of the site.

For that there are lots of stock libraries. Some of my favorites are iStock photos, Getty Images, and

Stocksy. These kinds of places sell very creative and high-quality, professional images you can use in your branding.

Even better than that, entrepreneurs need to invest in images of themselves. You will need photos for everything: when you do interviews, for your "About" page, your website, your social media profiles, your book cover, flyers, etc.

You need a nice head shot. Investing in one will make a huge difference for your business. You can use it anywhere, so choose a good photographer.

Make sure you ask some questions before signing a contract though. Some photographers charge for the shoot and give you only one photo, so make sure you know the terms of your agreement and actively participate in your shot.

Think through what you want to wear. When you think about your branding and how you want to present yourself, dress that way in your shots.

Photos are beautiful, and they should be used in moderation. Just slapping photos up is not enough. Also, on social media, using just any random, poor-quality quote that you just saw somewhere on Google search is not going to help at all, but a beautiful image will draw attention from social media and bring people back over to your site.

So great photos really are essential, including really good photos of your product. You could also have a 3D graphic created as a model so that it looks like a physical product because when it's digital, people can't hold it.

"Before" and "after" shots are a really good idea for photos too. For example, I build websites. I could take a "before" photo of what the website looked like before I started to work on it and then the new website after. The same thing could work for a personal stylist; she could use photos of her clients before and after she styled them. Also, using photos with testimonials is a good idea. It adds more credibility and builds trust because they all look like real people when you have a photo with the testimonials.

If you do not have photos, Illustrations can be a unique and fun way to add contrast and enhance the visual experience for visitors to your website.

Your Instant Insights...

- When you think about your branding and how you want to present yourself, think through what you want to wear.

- You need a nice head shot for your website, book, flyer, and social media profile.

- Invest in quality photos of yourself and stock images for promotions.

Newsletter & Email Marketing Strategies for Creating Expert Status

Email Marketing has become a staple in the online marketing world, because it works. Email is inexpensive to send and lands directly in the inbox of your potential buyers.

Since most people who visit your site will visit only once, it's important to offer a reason for them to leave their name and e-mail address so that you can get in touch with them. You don't want to put the burden on them to remember you're available for hire.

Imagine sending an email and filling your new program, or selling 50 copies of your book, or enrolling new coaching clients. That's the power of email marketing. When done correctly, your newsletter can be your website (and your business's) most powerful partner.

First you'll need to build a list of people who are interested in your services.

Email marketing an e-mail opt-in is essential. This is a form that you can put on your website to collect information, and you can customize the information that you collect. The most common form of opt-in is a simple form that asks for a name and e-mail address in exchange for a free gift.

The idea behind creating a free gift is that it should be something that is valuable to your ideal client. You want to give them something useful, something that gives them an idea of what it is like to work with you. That's why you want to give something of high quality.

I always say you want to create a free gift that you can actually charge for. I like to call it a "freemium" because it's not just something cheap that you throw up on your website. It should be something well thought-out, created with your audience in mind, and designed to lead them to the next step.

For example, I recently created an opt-in for a business owner who teaches systems and business automation. Her freemium opt-in gift was a Productivity Playbook, where she shares 3 of the most common mistakes her audience faces and provides insightful steps to help her reader. When you visit her website there's a web form to put in your name and e-mail address to receive her free gift.

The productivity tips all have actionable things you can do, and they move people into her introductory offering, which is to help entrepreneurs get more organized so that they can be productive. She shares the starter steps, the basic things her potential clients need to have in place before working with her.

You can use this same strategy in your business. What can you create that gives your audience an idea of what it's like to work with you? What will you offer the people who sign up for your free gift. Think about the things your clients need to have before they come to work with you.

Try to keep it simple and creative. Things like worksheets, eBooks, white papers, and other documents that can be created as PDFs are a great way to create a quick freemium that still adds tons of value.

With social media being so popular, what's the deal with the email craze? Wondering why you should spend any time at all creating something irresistible to your ideal clients just to give it away!

Call it an ethical bribe, a big banana, a pink spoon, your irresistible free offer (IFO), a lead magnet... the name isn't important, they all essentially work the same way. You create something of value, read great information and insight into what you offer the world for sale, and you give it away for FREE in exchange for the name and email of a potential client.

I'm sure you've signed up for at least one. You visit a website enter your name and email address and in return they send you a cute 'lil PDF, audio or video series.

It may seem counter-intuitive but think about it like this. You visit a website, you really like what they're offering... but you don't have the money right now, you're a little skeptical whether it will work for you or you're still in the researching stage.

Now as a customer you've likely been in one of those situations. As a business owner this is where your potential client is as well. Asking for the email address is a great way for you to be able to reach out again to them when they are ready, and to share your expertise and minimize their skepticism.

Getting an email address from a potential client is a privilege.

1. It's a sign of trust. An inbox is a personal thing. and when someone is willing to let you into theirs,

it's a big deal. Respect their trust by actually delivering on what you promised. Don't just send a thinly veiled sales pitch. People see right through that and your trust is broken already.

2. It means that what you offered them was GOOD and something they wanted to know more about. So don't be shy in inviting them to work with you. As long as the offer is relevant and comes with the value you promised. Your prospect will appreciate the opportunity to get their problem solved.

A Freebie or a Freemium as I like to call it. Is a special 'lil something, something you give away in exchange for the contact info of potential clients. Now you can't just throw up anything and expect to build your list...you need to be strategic about it. Ideally you will reverse engineer your service and create your Freemium as a teaser, or a taste of your full offering.

For example: I'm a website strategist + designer, I work with creative entrepreneurs to build a website that supports their empire. My Freemium is called Your Brand Map - 5 Steps to Website Clarity

Your Freemium can help people complete the step before they work with you, like mine.

It can also be the first step of your process. For example, is you're a coach, you can share the first step in your signature system. Or you can give short insight into each stage of your process.

Here are 12 Fresh ideas for your Freemium

1. A digital quiz

2. List of resources

3. Video series

4. Weekly Series

5. E-course

6. Personal time

7. Checklist

8. Webinar or Teleseminar

9. MP3

10. White paper or special report

11. An e-book

12. Pretty things - screen saver, photo, inspirational quote

Depending on your business and your intended audience you can come up with something that serves your clients and allows you to shine as the expert you are.

A free gift can come in many different formats. It can be an audio or a video, and even a video can be a screen share of a pdf with audio over it if you're a little shy over camera. You can do audio with a conference line or by recording yourself rather than making that live. Videos and video series are really popular for opt-ins remember to keep it simple and creative.

Planning Your Opt-in Sequence

Now let's talk about the entire sequence and how the opt-in sequence flow works. On your visitor's end, when they land on your website, they will see a web form that asks for a name and e-mail address. This is called an opt-in box. In your opt-in box you want to put a strong headline and an image or photograph of your "freemium" along with a descriptive bit of copy, perhaps a list of benefits as bullet points and a strong call to action to invite people to get your free gift.

The opt-in box is your web form and will allow people to enter their name and email address on your website.

1. Potential client enters their name and e-mail address into the opt-in box on your website.

2. Once they click the SEND button, two things can happen:

   a. Single Opt-In Sequence - a single opt-in, means that when potential clients click the SEND button, they'll be given immediate access to your free gift without confirming that the email they entered is correct.

b. Double Opt-In Sequence - a double opt-in sequence requires the potential client to check their email and click a confirmation link sent by your email service provider before they can access your free gift.

You do not have to manually do every time someone signs up for your newsletter. Your e-mail service provider will do this automatically; you just set it up within your chosen email service provider's system.

A word about opt-ins. Check your country's federal regulations for special requirements on the use of a single or a double opt in.

Your Instant Insights...

- Use a Freemium offer to compel potential clients to leave their name and e-mail address.
- Create a free gift so good you could actually charge for.
- Reverse-engineer your "freemium" to lead into your services.

Super Simple SEO

It never fails, someone always asks, "How do I get on the first page of Google?"

First, let me just say it's not impossible. The quickest way is to pay. Google runs a very respectable ads program, Google Ads. The other way is to blog. Google will give you über search engine points for creating useful content and regularly sharing it on your blog. Google understands how people search, by asking questions.

They understand how people use the Internet and reward content creators with great placement in search results. As a content creator, you can make it easy for Google and visitors to find you by using these super simple SEO techniques to optimize your website and blog posts.

Simple SEO

Select a keyword phrase (instead of a single keyword) and a few variations of your keyword phrase. Use only one keyword phrase per web page.

Use your keyword phrase in the following places on your site.

Your domain name or URL – www.yourwebsite. com/keyword-phrase

Title Tag – This is the place in the code that robots read. They look here to see what the page is about. It is fifty to seventy characters, so use your keyword phrase in the first five words. Each page on your site will need a unique title tag.

Description – This is the actual information that shows up in search results. You have 160 characters to entice readers to click.

- In the main heading (H1 tag or the post title)
- Subheadings (h2 and h3 tags)
- In the first paragraph
- Optimize your images—add an ALT Tag, Description, and Title for your image
- In a link (either to another article on your blog or from another article on your blog)

- Write a custom META DESCRIPTION that includes your keyword phrase
- Page Title
- Included throughout the article (for a 500-word post about five times throughout the post in various ways that still make sense to readers)

Your Instant Insights...

- The quickest way to get on the first page of Google is to pay.
- Blogging is the secret to search engine success.
- SEO can be simple.

Putting Together Your Website Strategy

We've talked branding, photos, web copy, and all things websites. Now let's put it all together and create your own strategic website plan.

Website Planning Checklist To-Do's:

- Purchase hosting and a domain name
- Have professional headshots taken
- Write your website content or hire a writer
- Secure your contact information, PO Box, 1-800 #, email address
- Purchase a photo credit package
- Decide on email service provider

- Collect testimonials

What You Need to Know

- Who is your ideal client?
- What do you offer, what services do you provide?
- What do you want visitors to do?
- What pages will you need?
- What kinds of Multi Media Needs do you have (Audio, Video, PDF)?

Questions Your Website Needs to Answer

- Who do you work with?
- What do you do for them?
- What's your process?
- How can they hire you?

About the Author

I began my entrepreneurial journey as a web and graphic designer making business cards and brochures to pay my way through college.

My major was journalism and mass media communication. I wanted to be a news anchor and live the glamorous life of a New York author and journalist, but God had a different plan. A good friend of mine, Amade, had gifted me an old Compaq computer (remember those?) with Photoshop on it. That's when the entrepreneurial bug bit me.

And ... I fell in love. I would sit at the computer for hours and hours designing. I created my own flyer and started taking on clients. Soon I had a full portfolio and a thriving lil business going.

Thirteen years later, that cute lil business is boomi1ng. Over the years I've had the pleasure of working with clients all over the United States and Canada as well as New Zealand, Australia, Tanzania, France, Argentina, and Sweden— all while working from home and raising my daughter.

It's life changing when you can make a living doing something you love from anywhere in the world.

It gives you options, choices, and a freedom like no other. I want that for anybody who wants it for themselves. I hope this book help you do that.

I believe in the power of marketing, technology, and entrepreneurship to make the world a better place, go do your part.

Connect with the Author

Website:
MelodyHunter.com

Email:
xo@MelodyHunter.com

Social Media:
Facebook: https://www.facebook.com/
MelodyeHunterCreativeMedia/

LinkedIn: https://www.linkedin.com/in/
melodyehunter

Twitter: https://twitter.com/melodyehunter

Instagram: https://www.instagram.com/
melodyehunter/

Pinterest: https://www.pinterest.com/
melodyehunter/

Google+: https://plus.google.com/+MelodyeHunter

Acknowledgements

I would like to thank Robbin Simons and the entire Crescendo Publishing Team.

Meriflor Toneatto, you have inspired me more than you know, thank you.

Dr. Venus Opal Reese, Sonaya Williams, DaRhonda Williams, and Dr. Takiyah Nur Amin, you ladies shine so bright I have to wear my shades in your presence! Thank you for shining so brightly that you've blazed a trail for me.

Lois, Sherrye, Vikkie, Keith, Michelle, Lawrence, Jerry, Dionne, Shamika, Jacinda, Reana, Jessica, Jason, Alyssa, Alfred, Isabelle, Donny, Keishawnda, Phillip, Zaria, Sheree, Morgan, Lawrence, Angelina, Marlayna, Curnelious, shine bright, Kierra and Marianna, you are all very special to me.

Dr. Dionna Hancock-Johnson, Erika Jones, Erica Aker, and Ravina Baskerville-Lottie, I love you.

Farod, I couldn't have completed this book without your love, thank you.

About Crescendo Publishing

Crescendo Publishing is a boutique-style, concierge VIP publishing company assisting entrepreneurs with writing, publishing, and promoting their books for the purposes of lead-generation and achieving global platform growth, then monetizing it for even more income opportunities.

Check out some of our latest best-selling AuthorPreneurs at http://CrescendoPublishing.com/new-authors/.

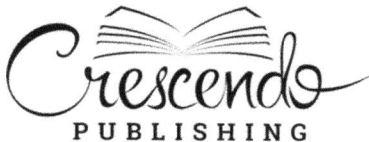

About the Instant Insights™ Book Series

The *Instant Insights™ Book Series* is a fact-only, short-read, book series written by EXPERTS in very specialized categories. These high-value, high-quality books can be produced in ONLY 6-8 weeks, from concept to launch, in BOTH PRINT & eBOOK Formats!

This book series is FOR YOU if:

- You are an expert in your niche or area of specialty

- You want to write a book to position yourself as an expert

- You want YOUR OWN book – NOT a chapter in someone else's book

- You want to have a book to give to people when you're speaking at events or simply networking

- You want to have it available quickly

- You don't have the time to invest in writing a 200-page full book

- You don't have a ton of money to invest in the production of a full book – editing, cover design, interior layout, best-seller promotion

- You don't have a ton of time to invest in finding quality contractors for the production of your book – editing, cover design, interior layout, best-seller promotion

For more information on how you can become an *Instant Insights™* author, visit **www.InstantInsightsBooks.com**

More Books in the
Instant Insight™ Series

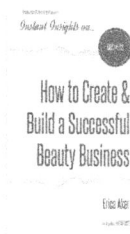

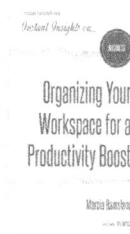

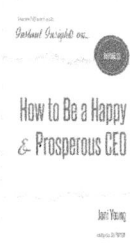

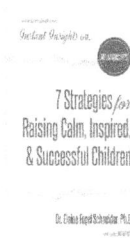

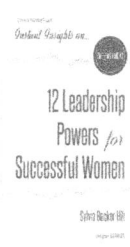

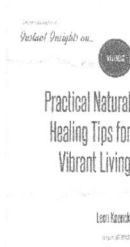

Instant Insights on...

A Time Management System for Creative Entrepreneurs

Maretha Reprelaar, Ph.D.

Instant Insights on...

Branding and Website Essentials for Entrepreneurs

Melody Marler

Instant Insights on...

How to Create & Build a Successful Beauty Business

Erica Allar

Instant Insights on...

Organizing Your Workspace for a Productivity Boost

Marcia Ramsland

Instant Insights on...

How to Be a Happy & Prosperous CEO

Jaki Young

Instant Insights on...

Taking Your Business from Startup to Thrive in 45 Days

Jodi Masters

Instant Insights on...

7 Strategies for Raising Calm, Inspired, & Successful Children

Dr. Enika Fogel-Schneidau, Ph.D.

Instant Insights on...

Creating a Solid, Lasting Connection with Your Kids

Dr. Vicki Panaccione

Instant Insights on...

12 Leadership Powers for Successful Women

Sylvia Becker-Hill

Instant Insights on...

MOTIVATION! Your Master Key to Success & Riches

Parviz Firouzgar

Instant Insights on...

PERFORMANCE POWER: Clarity, Confidence & Joy

Misty Mahoney

Instant Insights on...

Practical Natural Healing Tips for Vibrant Living

Leon Kanook

Crescendo
CrescendoPublishing.com

79

www.ingramcontent.com/pod-product-compliance
Lightning Source LLC
Chambersburg PA
CBHW060516280326
41933CB00014B/2986